# ELVIS®

# ELVIS®

## HIS LIFE IN PICTURES

A TINY FOLIO™

**ABBEVILLE PRESS · PUBLISHERS**

New York · London · Paris

# For the fans

Front cover: Elvis in a publicity photograph for his fourth film, *King Creole,* released in 1958.

Back cover: Elvis in concert, September 1956. See pages 48–49.

Spine: Elvis in a publicity photograph for *Flaming Star,* 1960.

Page 1: Elvis in the famous gold lamé suit, c. early 1957.

Page 2: Publicity photograph for *King Creole.*

Page 6: Elvis in a 1955 concert, probably in Tampa, Florida. This photograph was used on the cover of Elvis's first album, *Elvis Presley,* released in 1956.

Page 64: On a snowy March day in 1960 Elvis returns to civilian life after completing active army service. See page 87.

Page 94: Elvis in a publicity photograph for *Blue Hawaii.* See page 117.

Page 156: Performing in his 1968 television special "Elvis," taped in June of that year and broadcast in December.

Page 194: Detail of 1969 oil painting by Ralph Wolfe Cowan. See page 207.

Page 230: Graceland's entrance.

Page 272: Elvis in a thoughtful mood. This photograph was taken during sessions arranged in conjunction with his first post-army single, "Stuck on You," 1960.

*For copyright and Cataloging-in-Publication Data, see page 287.*

# CONTENTS

# EARLY YEARS AND
# MUSICAL BEGINNINGS
## 1935–1957

**E**lvis Aaron Presley was born in a two-room house in Tupelo, Mississippi, at 4:35 A.M. on Thursday, January 8, 1935, the second boy in a set of identical twins. The first, Jessie Garon, was stillborn. Elvis was the only child of Gladys Love Smith Presley and Vernon Elvis Presley. The Presleys and their relatives were a close-knit, hardworking family that attended the First Assembly of God Church, where young Elvis loved to sing gospel. He also grew up listening to the black bluesmen in the neighborhood and to country music on the radio.

(A note on the name: Elvis was named after his father, Vernon Elvis Presley, and Mr. Presley's good friend, Aaron Kennedy. "Aron" was the spelling the Presleys chose, apparently to make it similar to "Garon," the middle name of Elvis's twin. Toward the end of his life, Elvis sought to change the spelling of his middle name to the more traditional "Aaron." In the process he learned that official state records had inexplicably listed it as "Aaron" anyway, and not "Aron" as on his original birth records. "Aaron" is the spelling his family chose for his tombstone, and it has been designated the official spelling today by his estate.)

Early on, Elvis displayed notable singing talent. In the fall of 1945, ten-year-old Elvis entered a youth talent contest at the Mississippi-Alabama Fair & Dairy Show, which was held in Tupelo. He sang "Old Shep" and won the second place prize of $5.00 and free admission to all the fair's rides. Months later, Elvis received his first guitar, an inexpensive model purchased by his mother at the Tupelo Hardware Store. The Presley family lived in several different houses in Tupelo over the years, and Vernon and Gladys worked from job to job, trying to achieve a better standard of living. In late 1948, they packed all their belongings into their car and moved a couple of hours' drive north to Memphis, Tennessee, where they hoped to find greater opportunities.

Through much of Elvis's school years he and his parents lived in public housing in the poor neighborhoods of north Memphis. Elvis attended Humes High School and worked odd jobs to help support his family. The teenage Elvis bought his clothes on Beale Street—still popularly known as "The Home of the Blues"—and absorbed the black R & B and gospel music he heard there. He also attended all-night gospel sings downtown. He continued

Sun Studio owner/producer Sam Phillips shows Elvis a chord
in this posed shot at the Memphis studio, c. 1955.

to sing and play guitar, wore his hair long (by that day's standards) and slick, with sideburns. During his senior year at Humes High, Elvis won the annual school talent show, performing "Keep Them Cold Icy Fingers Off of Me" and receiving more applause than any other contestant.

After graduation on June 3, 1953, Elvis went to work at the Parker Machinists shop. That summer, Elvis took the first step toward becoming a professional singer when he stopped by Sun Records producer Sam Phillips's Memphis Recording Service. Phillips wasn't in, but his assistant Marion Keisker helped Elvis cut a $4.00 demo acetate record of "My Happiness" and "That's When Your Heartaches Begin." Elvis reportedly gave this record to his mother as an extra, belated birthday present (her birthday was April 25). Elvis then began driving a delivery truck for Crown Electric Company and attended electrician's school at night.

In January 1954 Elvis made another $4.00 acetate record at Sun. This time producer Sam Philips was in and seemed mildly interested in Elvis's raw talent. That summer Phillips was looking for a singer to record a new song called "Without You," and Marion Keisker remembered Elvis and suggested to Sam Phillips that he give him a chance at it. Elvis did not perform the tune to Phillips's satisfaction, but Phillips recognized an untapped talent.

Soon after, Elvis teamed up with local musicians Scotty Moore, who played guitar, and Bill Black, who played stand-up bass, and went to record again at Sun. On July 5, 1954, after a long day of mostly unsuccessful jamming, the guys broke into a sped-up version of Arthur Crudup's blues song "That's All Right, Mama" and everything clicked. Phillips was so impressed that he immediately recorded it, and later captured their up-tempo rendition of Bill Monroe's "Blue Moon of Kentucky" for the flip side of the single.

Phillips took acetates of Elvis's first commercial record around to local Memphis radio disc jockeys. WHBQ dj Dewey Phillips (no relation to Sam) played "That's All Right, Mama" on the radio on July 8. The phone rang off the hook with listener requests to hear it again and again, prompting Dewey to bring Elvis in that night for a live interview, and making him an overnight celebrity in Memphis. Sam Phillips signed Elvis to his first recording contract with Sun Records later that month.

Elvis, along with Scotty and Bill, began touring and making personal appearances around the South, supporting his eventual five Sun singles, which were all regional hits. Elvis's one appearance on the Grand Ole Opry that fall was met with a less than enthusiastic response, reportedly prompting talent coordinator Jim Denny to suggest that Elvis go back to driving a truck! But Elvis soon garnered a long-term performing contract with the *Louisiana Hayride*, a Saturday night country music radio show originating in

Shreveport, Louisiana, and broadcast over KWKH radio, an upstart competitor to Nashville's more established Grand Ole Opry radio program. During this time, drummer D. J. Fontana joined the band.

In the latter half of 1955, during the time he was appearing on *Louisiana Hayride,* Elvis met a promoter named Colonel Tom Parker. Parker became involved in Elvis's career and soon became his official and exclusive manager. (Scotty Moore had been the manager early on, followed by Bob Neal, who continued to consult for a while after Parker took over.) In the fall of 1955, Colonel Parker negotiated the sale of Elvis's Sun Records contract to RCA Records for a then-unprecedented $45,000. Elvis was definitely the hottest new star in the music business.

On January 10, 1956, two days after his twenty-first birthday, Elvis had his first recording session for RCA in their Nashville studios. "Heartbreak Hotel" was cut that day and released only weeks later, on January 27. It soon hit number one on Billboard's pop singles chart, staying in the top spot for eight weeks and becoming Elvis's first million-selling (or gold) single. The song also crossed over to hit number one on the country chart and top five on the rhythm & blues chart. In March, RCA released his first album, *Elvis Presley.* It soon found its way to Billboard's pop album chart, spending ten weeks at number one.

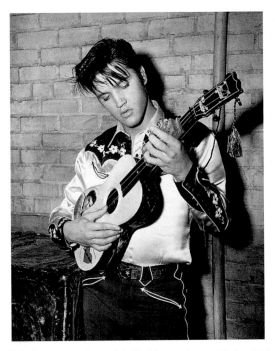

Elvis here wears the red-and-white cowboy outfit in which he sings "Teddy Bear" in the 1957 film *Loving You*. He strums an official toy Elvis guitar during a break in filming.

13

Elvis's network television career was launched on January 28, 1956, with the first of his six appearances on the Jackie Gleason–produced *Stage Show* variety program hosted by Tommy and Jimmy Dorsey on CBS. On April 3, 1956, Elvis made the first of his two appearances on *The Milton Berle Show* on ABC. On the second show, broadcast on June 5, he performed a sensuous, gyrating version of "Hound Dog," which, while in keeping with his usual live act, caused much consternation among adult viewers unfamilar with this young performer. Teenagers, of course, went wild with excitement. On July 1, 1956, Elvis (this time sedately attired in white tie and tails) did a tamer version of "Hound Dog" sung directly to a basset hound on NBC's *Steve Allen Show*. Finally, Elvis was invited by television's most popular variety show host, Ed Sullivan, to make three appearances on his program for a total of $50,000, at that time the largest sum ever paid to a television performer by far. On September 9, 1956, the first of these Sullivan appearances attracted fifty-four million viewers, then the largest television audience ever.

Motion pictures, too, beckoned this intriguing new star. Elvis had screen tested with Paramount in Hollywood in April 1956 and signed a seven-year movie contract with the studio. He shot his first movie in August, on loan from Paramount, with Twentieth Century Fox. *Love Me Tender* premiered on November 16, 1956, at the Paramount Theater in New York City and became a smash hit, as did the title song.

Meanwhile, Elvis continued to perform and make personal appearances all around the United States. His audiences grew bigger and bigger, wilder and wilder, increasing his fame. Colonel Parker developed souvenir Elvis merchandise including T-shirts, hats, belts, purses, jewelry, stuffed hound dogs, even a cologne. Elvis fans created pandemonium wherever he appeared. On January 6, 1957, two days before his twenty-second birthday, Elvis made his third and final appearance on *The Ed Sullivan Show*. This was the show that mandated the infamous "waist-up" camera angle, censoring Elvis's controversial pelvic and leg gyrations. Sullivan himself helped to defuse some of the controversy when he said on the air that "this is a real decent, fine boy" and that he had "never had a pleasanter experience on our show with a big name then we've had with you. You're thoroughly all right." High praise indeed from the man who had earlier remarked that Elvis "was not my cup of tea."

For Elvis, dubbed by the fans and media as the King of Rock & Roll, 1957 was another banner year. He continued touring and performing all over the United States, including Hawaii, plus five shows in three Canadian cities. That year he also filmed and released his second and third movies, *Loving You* and *Jailhouse Rock*, with accompanying hit sound-track recordings. In between career commitments,

Elvis managed to return to Memphis long enough to purchase Graceland in March 1957.

Celebrating his first Christmas at Graceland that December, Elvis received his official draft notice from the U. S. Army. His induction was postponed just long enough for him to complete filming his fourth motion picture, *King Creole*, considered by many to be his finest acting performance. His co-star Walter Matthau once said of Elvis, "He was an instinctive actor . . . very intelligent . . . he was not a punk. He was very elegant, sedate, and refined, and sophisticated." Elvis's star shone brightly over everything he tried: acting, singing, recording, and performing live. His next role, however, required only U.S. citizenship and "basic training."

Elvis's birthplace and first home in Tupelo, Mississippi.

Above: Elvis with his parents in Tupelo, c. 1937.
Opposite: A young Elvis.

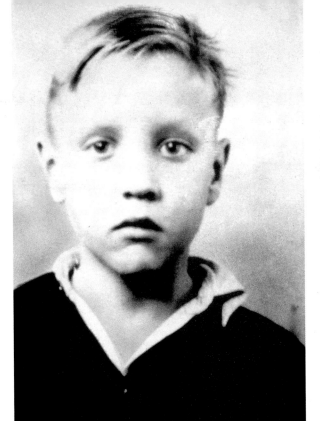

Elvis at grade school age with his parents.

At the Lauderdale Courts, Memphis, with a toy gun.

During his Humes High days.

23

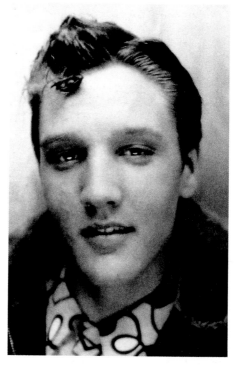

The legend takes shape: photos from the early fifties.

Above: A fresh-faced Elvis in 1955.
Opposite: Performing in 1955, probably at Fort Homer
Hesterly Auditorium, Tampa, Florida.

With the Jordanaires during a *Louisiana Hayride* performance. These shows were broadcast on KWKH Radio throughout the South, and helped the audience of the "Elvis Presley Show" to grow.

With bass player Bill Black and lead guitarist
Scotty Moore, c. 1955.

Performing on the *Louisiana Hayride* in
Shreveport, c. 1955–56.

An early publicity shot captures the Presley energy.

Elvis sings during a 1955 concert appearance.
Bassist Bill Black appears in the background.

Another 1955 show, most likely in Florida.

Elvis portrays
"relaxing at home"
for a fan magazine
photo, c. 1955–56.

Elvis signs autographs during the 1956 Presley for President campaign, more promotional than political.

Elvis in a promotional photograph with some friendly
"hound dogs."

Performing at the New Frontier Hotel, May 1956.
This was Elvis's first show in Las Vegas,
where he was billed as "The Atomic Powered Singer."
Scotty Moore is the lead guitarist.

Elvis is backed by the Jordanaires during
a 1957 concert.

An early performance, c. 1955.

In concert, c. early 1956.
Bass player Bill Black is in the background.

Elvis on stage in Memphis at a July 4, 1956, charity concert in Russwood Park. Independence Day that year was also declared Elvis Presley Day by the governor of Tennessee.

45

Concert appearance, c. 1956.

Elvis performing with the Jordanaires at the Mississippi-Alabama Fair in his hometown of Tupelo, Mississippi, September 26, 1956.

At the Mississippi-Alabama Fair in Tupelo, Mississippi, September 26, 1956. Elvis's parents were in the audience for this special homecoming performance. Eleven years earlier he had won second prize performing "Old Shep" in a youth talent contest at this same fair.

On set during the filming of *Love Me Tender*,
late summer 1956.

Elvis in the famed gold lamé suit designed by Nudie's of Hollywood and introduced to audiences in early 1957. This photograph adorns the album *50,000,000 Elvis Fans Can't Be Wrong, Elvis' Gold Records, Vol. 2,* released in 1959.

Elvis performed in the full gold suit only twice, on March 28, 1957, in Chicago and the next night in St. Louis. There are many different accounts of why he switched to wearing only the jacket: overzealous fans stormed the stage; the pants ripped; the suit shed gold when Presley hit the floor; the suit was hot and uncomfortable; and perhaps Elvis thought it a bit much. 53

A 1957 concert at Hollywood's Pan Pacific Auditorium,
where he played on October 28 and 29. He is now
performing with only the gold jacket, not the full suit.

Elvis from the same Hollywood 1957 concert,
here getting to know RCA spokesdog Nipper.

Elvis at the piano in a 1957 concert appearance.

Elvis caught mid-gyration in an April 1957 performance, one of his first in Canada.

Holding a press conference associated with one
of his 1957 concert appearances.

Relaxing during the filming of
*Jailhouse Rock*, 1957.

Performing in a benefit concert at the
Mississippi-Alabama Fair in Tupelo on
September 27, 1957.

A quiet moment during the same benefit
concert in Tupelo.

Elvis in early 1958 enjoying recording sessions associated with the film *King Creole*.

# THE ARMY YEARS
## 1958–1960

**O**n March 24, 1958, Elvis was inducted into the U.S. Army at the Memphis Draft Board. On March 25, at Fort Chaffee, Arkansas, he received his indoctrination exam and famous haircut, and was then assigned to basic training at Fort Hood, Texas. Private Presley was stationed there for six months, and his parents joined him at a temporary home near the base.

In August 1958, Gladys Presley became ill with acute hepatitis and returned to Memphis to be hospitalized. Elvis was granted emergency leave and arrived in Memphis on the afternoon of August 12. Gladys Presley died in the early hours of August 14 at the age of forty-six. She lay in state at Graceland, and services were held at the Memphis Funeral Home on August 15. Elvis was devastated by his mother's passing, but had to return to his army duties on August 25.

Elvis left the United States for an eighteen-month assignment in West Germany in September. His father, Vernon, and grandmother Minnie Mae Presley lived with him at his off-base residence in Bad Nauheim. It was there, in late 1959, that Elvis met Priscilla Ann Beaulieu, an American air force captain's daughter who would later play a significant role in his life and legacy. During this time Elvis also traveled to Paris on leave, visiting such nightspots as the Folies-Bergère and the Moulin Rouge.

Elvis was honorably discharged on March 5, 1960, having achieved the rank of sergeant. Elvis did not perform in concert during his two years in service, though he was often asked to do so. Although he worried intensely that so much time away from entertaining and moviemaking might destroy his career, he needn't have been concerned.

He returned to America's television screens on May 8, 1960, looking sharp and singing a duet with Frank Sinatra on a Timex/Sinatra television special. February 25, 1961, was declared Elvis Presley Day in Tennessee, and after a press luncheon in Memphis, Elvis gave two shows at Ellis Auditorium benefiting a long list of Memphis charities. And on March 25, 1961, he performed live before six thousand fans at Bloch Arena in Honolulu, in a benefit concert to raise money for a memorial to the USS *Arizona,* sunk at Pearl Harbor. Little did those fans know then that he would not perform live again until 1968. Hollywood continued to beckon.

Private Presley.

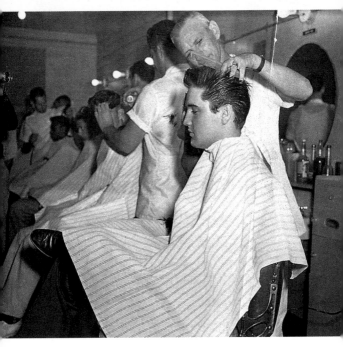

Elvis receives his GI haircut on March 25, 1958,
at Fort Chaffee, Arkansas; James Peterson is the barber.

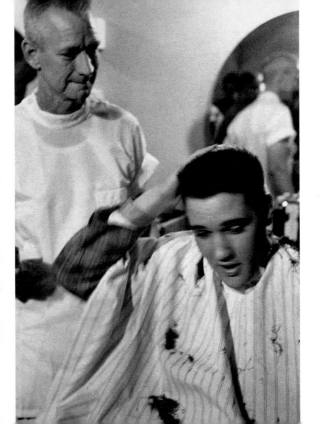

Elvis in front of Graceland, home while on leave from the army, June 1958.

Above and opposite: Elvis at home during his
June 1958 leave.

This shot was taken on the Graceland driveway.

74

Elvis took his army duties seriously, but also found time
to listen to music.

Elvis, at ease.

Taking a musical break from army life, c. 1959.
Elvis did not perform professionally during his time
in the army.

On maneuvers in Germany, c. 1958–59.

On maneuvers in Germany, c. 1958–59.

Army portrait, 1958.

Officer Presley in Germany, c. 1959.

Elvis in Paris on leave from the army, c. early 1960.

Soldier boy in transit, heading home during his
final days in the service.

Back from Germany, Elvis waves to fans after landing at McGuire Air Force Base in New Jersey on March 3, 1960, having completed active army service.

Above: Elvis with *(from left)* Joey Bishop, Frank Sinatra,
Nancy Sinatra, and Sammy Davis Jr. during the March 26, 1960,
taping of a Timex television special hosted by Mr. Sinatra.
The show was broadcast on May 8.
Opposite: Performing in the Timex/Sinatra television special.

Elvis turns it on for the Memphis crowd at Ellis Auditorium
on February 25, 1961, in one of two concerts that benefited
a number of local charities.

Above: Elvis arrives at Honolulu airport, March 25, 1961, in advance of that evening's benefit concert to aid the fund drive for a USS *Arizona* memorial.
Opposite: Checking the view before the concert, Elvis's last live performance for seven years.

# ELVIS IN HOLLYWOOD
## 1956–1969

**E**lvis starred in four films between 1956 and 1958, before he entered the army. They were wildly successful and are considered among the best he made. He went on to star in twenty-seven more feature films as an actor, beginning with 1960's *G. I. Blues,* made just after his release from the service, and ending with *Change of Habit* in 1969. The sound track to *G. I. Blues* went to number one on the Billboard album chart for ten weeks, staying on the chart for a total of 111 weeks, the longest chart listing of any Elvis recording. Elvis also starred in two theatrically released concert documentary films, *Elvis— That's the Way It Is* in 1970 and *Elvis on Tour* in 1972.

The marketing plan devised by Colonel Parker for Elvis in the 1960s did not include live performances; these would divert valuable attention away from the movies, which were coming out at a rate of two or three a year. Most of Elvis's recorded material released in the sixties appeared as movie sound tracks, although there were also a few regular LPs and greatest hits packages, and two gospel albums. (Elvis received his first Grammy Award for his work on the 1967 gospel album *How Great Thou Art.*)

The films and film-related records were wonderfully successful, but as the decade wore on, these projects, though still profitable, were not nearly as successful as they had been. The public was growing weary of the "Presley formula." The weariest of all was Elvis himself, supremely frustrated and unhappy with the state of his career. He had hoped to become a serious actor, but Hollywood had other ideas and Elvis had gone along with them.

Of course life wasn't entirely formulaic. One of the happiest events in Elvis's life occurred on May 1, 1967, when he and Priscilla Ann Beaulieu were married at the Aladdin Hotel in Las Vegas. Priscilla and Elvis had met through an acquaintance in the fall of 1959 during his army stint in West Germany. The couple honeymooned for a few days in Palm Springs, California, before returning to Memphis. On May 29, 1967, they donned their wedding clothes again and had a reception in the trophy room at Graceland for family and friends in Memphis. Nine months to the day after their wedding, on February 1, 1968, Priscilla gave birth to their first and only child, Lisa Marie.

And Elvis's greatest successes were still ahead.

Publicity photograph for *Love Me Tender*, 1956.

Publicity photographs taken in connection with Elvis's first film, *Love Me Tender*, which premiered in New York City, November 16, 1956.

Autographed publicity photo, 1956.

Elvis in his second film, *Loving You,* which premiered in Memphis, July 9, 1957.

Elvis in *Loving You*, 1957.

Above: Promotional photograph related to Elvis's third
film, *Jailhouse Rock,* released in November 1957.
Opposite: Elvis during a break in the filming of
*Jailhouse Rock,* 1957.

Publicity photos for *King Creole*, 1958.

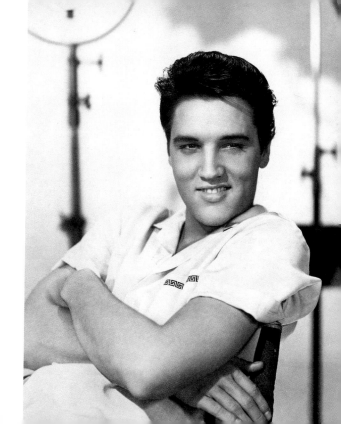

Publicity photos for *King Creole,* 1958.

A still photograph from Elvis's first
post-army film, *G. I. Blues*, 1960.

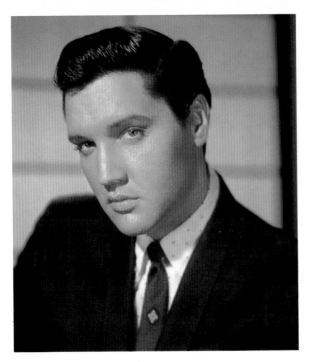

Image from a 1962 photo session.

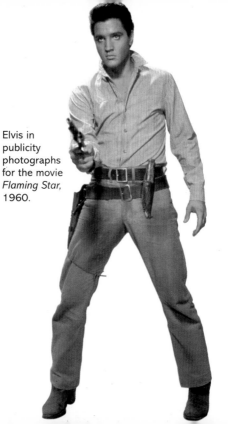

Elvis in publicity photographs for the movie *Flaming Star*, 1960.

Rehearsing lines and relaxing on the set of *Flaming Star*.

Elvis in publicity photographs for the movie
*Blue Hawaii,* 1961. The shot of Elvis in a Hawaiian shirt
was used for the cover of the sound-track album, one of
Elvis's most successful.

117

Photographs from the film *Kid Galahad*, 1962.

Above: Elvis in *Girls! Girls! Girls!*, part of which was filmed
in Hawaii in 1962.
Opposite: A still from *It Happened at the World's Fair*,
released in 1963.

Images from *Fun in Acapulco,* 1963.

Above: Shot from a publicity photo session, 1964.
Opposite: Promotional image for *Viva Las Vegas*,
124          released in 1964.

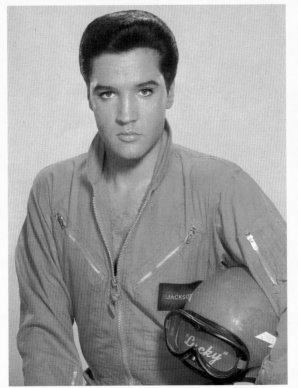

Images associated with *Roustabout*, one of four Elvis films released in 1964.

Elvis in stills from *Tickle Me*, filmed in 1964–65.

In costume for the 1965 film *Harum Scarum*.

On the set of *Frankie and Johnny* during the 1965 filming.

Promotional shot from c. 1965–66.

Elvis takes a break during the filming of
*Paradise, Hawaiian Style,* 1965.

A still from *Paradise, Hawaiian Style,* which was partially filmed in Hawaii and released in 1966.

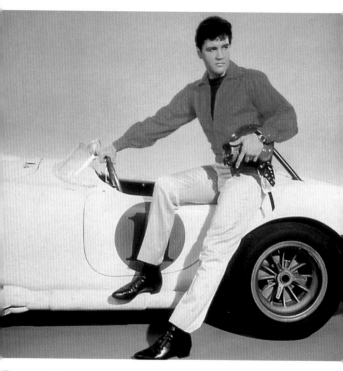

Elvis in publicity photographs for the movie *Spinout*, 1966.

Taking a rare turn at the drums in a
publicity photo for *Spinout*.

A still from *Spinout*.

Elvis and Priscilla were married on May 1, 1967,
at the Aladdin Hotel in Las Vegas.

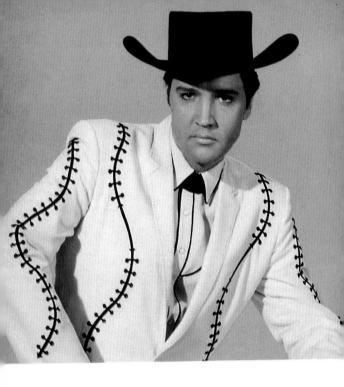

142

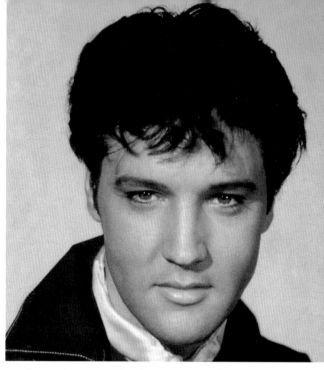

Images from promotional photo sessions for *Clambake*, released in 1967 and Elvis's twenty-fifth film.

Elvis in Arizona during the filming of
*Stay Away, Joe,* 1968.

Elvis during the filming of *Stay Away, Joe*.

In *Speedway,* released in 1968. These photos appear
on the cover of the sound-track album.

Elvis in *Charro!*, 1969.

In costume for the 1969 film *The Trouble with Girls*
*(and How to Get Into It)*.

With a koala bear received during the production of
*The Trouble with Girls.*

Elvis's final acting performance came in the 1969 movie *Change of Habit*, his thirty-first film.

# THE COMEBACK
## 1968 and Beyond

It was the summer of 1968. Elvis had last appeared in front of a live audience seven years earlier at the USS *Arizona* benefit show in Hawaii. In June 1968, Elvis taped a television special called "Elvis," which aired on NBC in December. The landmark show featured Elvis jamming informally and reminiscing with former bandmates Scotty Moore and D. J. Fontana (Bill Black had since died), and several longtime friends.

In other sequences, Elvis took the stage alone, in the center of a crowd of young fans, and performed many of his greatest rock & rollers and ballads. He introduced new songs that became classics, such as "Memories." There was also a gospel production number. Another segment of the show portrayed Elvis's own career, tracing a young man's journey from a struggling guitar player ("Guitar Man"), through all the challenges ("Big Boss Man"), dangers ("Trouble"), and compromises faced on the path to satisfying his dreams of success and superstardom. But something is lost along the way. Once the dream is achieved, the man realizes that he remains unfulfilled, that he has abandoned his "true self," to whom he finally returns. The 1968 special represents Elvis's own return to his true self.

At the end of the special, Elvis appears alone to sing a brand-new song, specially written for the show, called "If I Can Dream." The writer had created it based on conversations with Elvis about his thoughts on what was happening in the turbulent sixties, his feelings about life, and his hopes for humankind. It represents one of the few times Elvis would sing a secular "message" song, and his passionate performance of it is astounding.

Elvis clearly poured years of pent-up creative energy and passion into this show. His natural talent, charisma, and sensuality had not been diminished by Hollywood or by the passage of time. In fact, Elvis looked, sounded, moved, and grooved better than he ever had. At thirty-three, he was better than anybody in the business.

In January and February 1969, fresh from the success of his television special, Elvis recorded in Memphis for the first time since 1955, putting in several marathon sessions at American Sound Studio. These sessions resulted in such brilliant hits as "Suspicious Minds," "In the Ghetto," and "Kentucky Rain." On July 31, 1969, Elvis opened at the International Hotel in Las Vegas (renamed the Hilton in 1971) for a four-week, fifty-seven-performance engagement that broke Las Vegas concert attendance records. He broke his own record there with another engagement in February 1970, and followed this with a wonderfully successful six-show engagement at the Houston Astrodome. The six Astrodome performances attracted a record-breaking 207,494 people.

When Elvis returned to Vegas in the summer, MGM filmed a critically acclaimed documentary, *Elvis—That's the Way It Is,* released to theaters later that year. During the fall of 1970, Elvis took his concert show on the road, his first tour since 1957. In 1971, Elvis received the "Ten Outstanding Young Men of the Nation" award from the Jaycees, saw the stretch of Highway 51 South running in front of Graceland become Elvis Presley Boulevard, and received a lifetime achievement Grammy Award.

In 1971 and 1972, his engagements in Las Vegas continued to be standing room only, and his fast-paced concert tours across the nation continued to attract sell-out crowds and critical acclaim. MGM followed his spring 1972 tour, filming a second documentary, *Elvis on Tour,* which won a Golden Globe Award. In June 1972, Elvis was booked into Madison Square Garden in New York City, making history there with four sold-out shows attended by fans such as John Lennon, George Harrison, Bob Dylan, David Bowie, and Art Garfunkel.

It was a thrilling time in Elvis's career, but it was also during this time that his marriage to Priscilla was ending. It is said that his poignant recordings of "Always on My Mind" and "Separate Ways" in 1972 reflected his emotional state following their separation earlier that year. "Burning Love," however, which went to number two on the pop chart in 1972, seemed indicative of the state of his career—HOT!

Elvis next made television and entertainment history with his "Elvis—Aloha from Hawaii, via Satellite" special. It took place at the Honolulu International Center Arena on January 14, 1973. The show was broadcast live at 12:30 A.M. Hawaiian time, beamed via Globecam Satellite to Australia, South Korea, Japan, Thailand, the Philippines, South Vietnam, and several other countries. A tape of the show was seen in America on April 4 on NBC, attracting 51 percent of the television viewing audience. It was seen in more American households than the live broadcast of man's first walk on the moon. In all, it was seen in about forty countries by approximately one and a half billion people. Never had one performer held the world's attention in such a way. The sound-track album went to number one on the Billboard pop album chart in 1973, and stayed on the chart at various positions for a year.

This concert probably marks the pinnacle of Elvis's superstardom. In fact, he redefined the term *superstar*. Looking back at the footage and photos from this remarkable moment in history, it is hard to believe that Elvis, who was so magnificent in the show, in fine form physically and vocally, would die a little over four and a half years later. After "Aloha," the decline in his health and personal happiness became evident.

Of course, sellout crowds still clamored to see him in

person. In Pontiac, Michigan, at the newly opened Silver-dome, Elvis set a single performance attendance record of 62,500 people on New Year's Eve, December 31, 1975. In 1976, Elvis toured extensively; the year was also marked by his continued engagements in Las Vegas and the famous recording sessions conducted in his den at Graceland in February and October.

Between January and June 1977 alone Elvis gave fifty-five shows, despite increasing health problems and hospitalizations for a wide array of illnesses and pre-scription drug dependency. In June, during Elvis's last time out on the road, shows in Omaha and Rapid City were filmed in preparation for an upcoming CBS televi-sion special, "Elvis in Concert." His last performance was on June 26, 1977, at Market Square Arena in Indianapo-lis, Indiana.

In July, Elvis was named Favorite Rock Music Star and Favorite Variety Star by *Photoplay* magazine. The next leg of Elvis's 1977 concert touring schedule was to begin on Wednesday, August 17, in Portland, Maine, and conclude ten cities later back in Memphis. At that time, it is said that Elvis had talked about slowing down his touring and seek-ing out new film projects—movies that he would find chal-lenging and in which he could prove himself as an actor. We will never know exactly what his plans were or what might have been the next exciting chapter in his life and career. He died of heart failure on August 16, 1977.

Performing his hits in the 1968 special.

Performing the opening song of the 1968 special.

Two shots from the 1968 television special.
Above: Elvis performing the show's gospel medley.
Opposite: Elvis in a scenario from the semi-
autobiographical production number.

Elvis during the informal jam session.

Singing "If I Can Dream," the finale of the
television special "Elvis."

Elvis returned to performing live with a vengeance in the summer of 1969. He is shown here during his four-week engagement at the International Hotel, Las Vegas, the first of many such extended hotel dates.

Performing during one of his two International Hotel engagements in 1970. Part of the first gig was recorded and resulted in the live album *On Stage—February 1970*.

A happy moment at a press conference and a Texas welcome:
At the Houston Astrodome in 1970 Elvis performed six times
in three days (two shows each on February 22, February 28,
and March 1) before a total of 207,494 people.

WELCOME TO HOUSTON...
ELVIS...ELVIS...ELVIS...EL
ELVIS...ELVIS...ELVIS.
ELVIS...ELVIS...ELVIS...EL
ELVIS...ELVIS...ELVIS
ELVIS...ELVIS...ELVIS...EL

On December 21, 1970, Elvis paid a surprise visit to the White House, and eventually greeted President Nixon in person. Elvis was presented with a federal badge.

A seemingly nonpartisan Elvis is shown here meeting with Jimmy and Rosalyn Carter in the mid-seventies, when Carter was governor of Georgia.

In September 1970 Elvis embarked on his first concert tour since 1957, a brief but highly successful six-city run that crisscrossed the country. He toured again in November, hitting eight western cities in nine days. These photographs capture Elvis during this period.

For much of his adult life Elvis pursued a strong interest in
karate (left), and incorporated karate moves into his stage act,
as he does here in a 1971 Las Vegas performance (above).

Elvis toured twice in spring 1972, once in April and again in
June. The second tour took off from New York after his four
record-setting sellout shows at Madison Square Garden.
These images are from this period of touring.

179

The April 1972 concerts were filmed for the documentary *Elvis on Tour*. These shots were taken during that run.

More concert photos from 1972, during the period
in which *Elvis on Tour* was filmed.

Elvis live on stage, 1972.

Elvis played more than a thousand shows between 1970 and 1977, and adopted a number of different stage looks. Here are two outfits from the early seventies.

Arriving in Hawaii before the big concert, January 1973.

The 1973 TV special "Elvis—Aloha from Hawaii, via Satellite"
was seen by more than one billion people in forty countries—
the largest audience ever for such an event.

Elvis during the "Aloha from Hawaii,
via Satellite" television special, January 14, 1973.

All proceeds from the sale of tickets and merchandise
at this concert and the rehearsal show went to the
Kui Lee Cancer Fund.

On stage in the mid-seventies.

Elvis in concert, c. 1976. This photograph was used for the cover of Elvis's second-to-last album, *From Elvis Presley Boulevard, Memphis, Tennessee, 1976,* recorded in the Jungle Room den at Graceland.

# SOMETHING FOR
# EVERYBODY
## Memories and Memorabilia

**I**t is safe to say that Elvis and Colonel Tom Parker blazed new trails in the area of celebrity merchandising. Almost from the very beginning there was an unending demand for Elvis merchandise, and in response fans were treated to Elvis posters and trading cards, lipstick and jewelry, and shoes, purses, and wallets, in addition to the steady stream of movies and music.

Over the course of Elvis's career there were ample opportunities for promoting the singer, and Parker was a master at it. From the Presley for President campaign of 1956 to the post-army film *G. I. Blues* to the unprecedented "Aloha from Hawaii" spectacle, there was always a plan to attract attention. Through it all Elvis was unstintingly respectful of his fans, never forgetting their loyalty, and in turn the fans continued to clamor for anything and everything Elvis.

Of course, Elvis did his own share of collecting, as is made apparent on a tour of Graceland. Beyond the awards and gold records presented to Elvis, the trophy building and other exhibits contain evidence of many other Presley passions. There are outfits from Elvis's movie roles and many of the celebrated jumpsuits from his seventies tours; Elvis's large collection of guns and law enforcement badges; records by some of Elvis's favorite artists; and paintings, plaques, and photographic greetings from the fans.

One of the most impressive collections at Graceland is housed in the Elvis Presley Automobile Museum. Here more than twenty vehicles compete for attention, and beyond the well-known Cadillacs and Stutzes there is also a variety of unique "moto-toys": three-wheeled cycles, a golf cart, and even a grass-converted snowmobile. To accommodate his extensive touring schedule in 1975, Elvis made the ultimate transportation purchase when he bought two planes, the first in April and a second in September. He spent more than two million dollars on the two aircraft, a clear indication that he had fully overcome his early fear of flying. The larger and more lavish of the two, the *Lisa Marie,* he named in honor of his daughter.

Promotional material for *King Creole,* 1958.

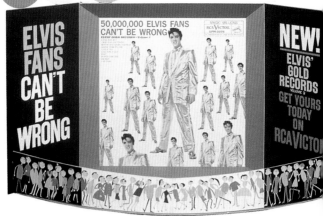

Above: Stand-up display for Elvis's second collection of gold records, *50,000,000 Elvis Fans Can't Be Wrong.*
Opposite: Teens could keep Elvis always on their lips with this "excitingly alive" Elvis Presley lipstick.

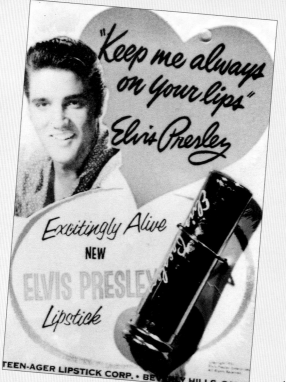

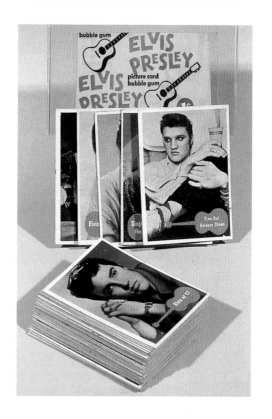

Above: Early merchandise catering to the female fan:
makeup case, purse, wallet, pins, and ID bracelets.
Opposite: Elvis bubble gum trading cards, a notion
initiated in 1956.

Holding a plastic toy Elvis guitar. This photograph was taken during a break in the filming of *Loving You*, 1957.

The complete collection of guitars at Graceland, set up for this photo on the front stairs of the house. A violin occasionally played by Elvis (not on stage) is included.

Promotional album "suitcases" for the film
*Fun in Acapulco*, which was released in 1963.

Some of Elvis's jewelry (clockwise from top center): gold cross pendant encrusted with small diamonds, a 1973 Christmas gift; gold TCB ring made in 1975; gold award belt presented to Elvis in 1969 by the International Hotel in Las Vegas; gold Rolex watch presented to Elvis by officials of the Houston Astrodome in 1970; gold Elvis pendant, a gift from the Kui Lee Cancer Fund in appreciation of the 1973 "Aloha from Hawaii" concert (he wore the pendant during the show); gold ID bracelet, given to Elvis by his entourage (each member of which had received one from him); gold karate ring, given by karate instructor Ed Parker in recognition of Elvis' reaching eighth-degree black belt; gold-and-diamond *chai* pendant.

Oil painting by Ralph Wolfe Cowan made in 1969.
Elvis paid $10,000 for the life-size portrait and $8,000 for
the foreign and U.S. copyrights, the only painting he ever
commissioned. The original hangs in the trophy building
today, as it did in Elvis's lifetime.

Suit from the gospel portion of the 1968 television special,
shown on display at Graceland.

Black leather suit, also from the 1968 special.

Cape from c. 1973.

Cape that Elvis wore in the 1973 "Aloha from Hawaii"
concert and which he tossed into the audience at the end
of the show. It was recovered by Graceland in 1995.

Jumpsuit with red and yellow rhinestones worn in concert by Elvis, c. 1973–74.

Blue "claw" outfit worn by Elvis in 1975.

Front and back views of the American eagle jumpsuit worn
during the 1973 "Aloha from Hawaii" concert.

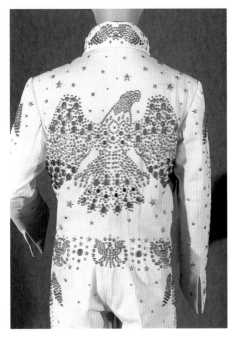

Elvis told his designer Bill Belew he wanted something that would say "America" to his international television audience.

Above: The 1955 pink Cadillac, Elvis's mother's favorite, in front of Graceland.
Opposite: Elvis driving through the Graceland gates in the early sixties.

Originally white,
this 1956 Cadillac convertible
was painted purple at Elvis's request.

Elvis's 1956 Continental Mark II, shown in the automobile museum at Graceland.

Elvis purchased this Willys jeep in 1960; the Graceland
security staff used it to patrol the grounds.

Four of Elvis's many motorcycles, photographed in
the automobile museum (from left):
1966 Harley-Davidson chopper; 1965 Honda, and
two 1976 Harley-Davidson Electra-Glide 1200 bikes.

Elvis takes a spin in one of his three-wheeled vehicles,
c. 1975–76.

The 1975 Dino Ferrari 308 GT4 Coupe.

A special favorite, the 1973 Stutz Blackhawk. When Elvis drove home through the gates of Graceland for the last time, on August 16, 1977, he was at the wheel of this car.

Elvis bought this Convair 880 in 1975 for
touring, and dubbed it the *Lisa Marie*. The
letters TCB and lightning bolt on the tail

symbolize Elvis's motto for himself and
his entourage throughout the seventies:
"Taking care of business in a flash."

Private bedroom of the *Lisa Marie*.

The *Hound Dog II*, a Lockheed JetStar that
Elvis purchased in September 1975.

# LIFE AT GRACELAND
## 1957—1977

**W**hen Elvis was young, he would often tell his parents that some day he would make a lot of money, buy them the finest house in town, and end their years of hard work and financial struggle. On March 26, 1957, at the age of twenty-two, Elvis made good on that promise when he purchased Graceland Mansion for $100,000. The emerging King of Rock & Roll now had his castle.

Graceland began as a 500-acre farm owned by the S. E. Toof family. In 1939, a southern colonial mansion was commissioned by Ruth Brown Moore and her husband Dr. Thomas Moore, to be built on part of this land. Mrs. Moore's great-aunt was the Grace in "Graceland," the name of the original farm. The new house took on the same name. In October 1940, a reporter from the Memphis Commercial Appeal wrote, "Located well back from Highway 51 in a grove of towering oaks, it stands proudly on land that has been in the family nearly a century. As you roll up the drive, you sense its fine heritage of the past in its general feeling of aristocratic kindliness and tranquillity." The feeling is much the same today.

Many additions and changes were made to the mansion and grounds during Elvis's years at Graceland, including the incorporation of trendy fifties, sixties, and seventies decor. Even though the estate was guarded and the house intended as a refuge from the world's attention, Elvis loved showing people his home. There were never any organized tours as there are today, but Elvis's family and friends recall his always saying to others, "Come to Memphis, I want to show you Graceland." Elvis is thus regarded as Graceland's original tour guide.

Today's tour guides show over 700,000 visitors a year things that Elvis included on his standard tour. The second floor of the mansion, which contains Elvis's private bedroom, wardrobe room, bath, and office; Lisa Marie's bedroom and bath; and an additional bath and dressing room, is not part of the tour.

There is much to see at Graceland today. Along with a monumental body of films, concert videos, recordings, and photographs, the history housed within the walls of Graceland preserves the memory of Elvis Aaron Presley for millions of devoted fans all over the world.

The front of Graceland at dusk.

The famous
front gates at
3764 Elvis
Presley
Boulevard,
added by
Elvis during
his first year
at Graceland.

Elvis always liked to give the house and grounds the full holiday treatment at Christmas, and the Graceland staff continues that tradition today.

The front stairs, just inside the front door at Graceland.

In front of the house with an unidentified
associate, 1957.

Elvis playing a bass guitar in the living room, 1963.

The living room and music room as seen from the front hall.
Though the peacock windows were added by Elvis in 1974,
the furnishings are largely those of an earlier design scheme.

In the music room, c. 1963. These red draperies were
usually in place for the Christmas season.

Inside the music room. Elvis replaced the white baby grand piano shown at left with this black baby grand in 1974.

Above: The dining room is on the opposite side of the front hall from the living room.
Opposite: The dining room, foyer, and living room, as seen from Elvis's usual seat at the table.

The tree as it was set up in the dining room, recreated here by the current Graceland staff.

The kitchen has been left as Elvis last decorated it in the mid-seventies. For Elvis, his family, and friends, it was a center of activity.

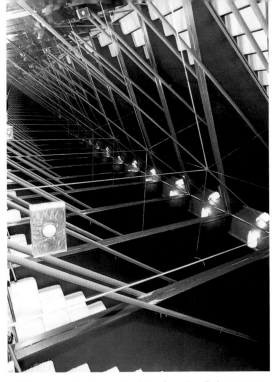

This mirrored stairway leads to Graceland's basement.

Two views of the TV room in the basement, as it looked since Elvis had it redecorated in 1974. Note the lightning bolt on the wall, a reference to Elvis's motto, "Taking care of business in a flash."

General view of the pool room, which Elvis also had redecorated in 1974.

253

This first-floor den, affectionately dubbed the Jungle Room by the public, was added by Elvis in the mid-sixties. The room was in fact an ordinary family room until Elvis redecorated in the mid-seventies. In 1976 Elvis made several recordings here.

255

Vernon Presley's office, located just behind the house.
The fan mail and household bills were handled here.

Lisa Marie's swing set sits just outside the front of the office.

The backyard.

Two horses in the pasture at Graceland.
The stables can be seen in the background.

Until the mid-sixties, Elvis's horseback riding was mostly limited to movie scenes. But after presenting Priscilla with a horse in 1966, he enthusiastically took up riding himself, and would sometimes trot out to the gate or front wall to greet fans and sign autographs.

261

A Presley
family
portrait,
c. 1971.

The hall of gold located in the trophy building, which was commissioned by Elvis to house his collection of awards and mementos.

The lower-level lounge in the racquetball building,
which Elvis built in 1975 to accommodate his new interest
in the sport. On the morning of August 16, 1977,
hours before his death, Elvis played his last few songs
at this piano.

The "wall of gold," mounted in the racquetball building and presented to the Elvis Presley Estate in August 1992 by RCA and the Recording Industry Association of America. It recognizes every Elvis album or single that ever went gold, platinum, or multi-platinum in America. There are 111 different albums with this distinction so far.

The Presley monument at the meditation garden, moved to this spot in 1977 from the family plot at Forest Hill Cemetery. The garden was constructed for Elvis in the mid-sixties as a place of refuge and peace.

A close view of the garden and fountain.

Elvis, his mother and father, and grandmother Minnie Mae
Presley are all buried at this site.

# CHRONOLOGY

**1935**   January 8—Elvis Aaron Presley is born in Tupelo, Mississippi.

**1948**   The Presley family moves to Memphis.

**1953**   Elvis graduates from Humes High School. During the summer Elvis records a demo acetate of "My Happiness" and "That's When Your Heartaches Begin" at the Memphis Recording Service (home of Sun Records).

**1954**   In July Sun Records owner/producer Sam Phillips brings Elvis together with two local musicians, guitarist Scotty Moore and bass player Bill Black. On July 5 the trio records "That's All Right, Mama," which, backed with the trio's "Blue Moon of Kentucky," is released on the Sun label on July 19. It is Elvis's first record release. The three continue to record and begin performing throughout the region.

**1955**   Drummer D. J. Fontana joins the band. Colonel Tom Parker becomes Elvis's manager. In November, Elvis signs with RCA Records, his label for the rest of his recording career.

**1956**   "Heartbreak Hotel," Elvis's first RCA single (and first gold record), is released in January. In March his first album, *Elvis Presley,* is released. He makes his first network television appearance on Stage Show, and later in the year appears on *The Milton Berle Show, The Steve Allen Show,* and *The Ed Sullivan Show*. In November Elvis's first movie, *Love Me Tender,* premieres in New York City.

**1957** In March Elvis buys Graceland. Both *Loving You* and *Jailhouse Rock* open this year. In November Elvis performs shows in Hawaii for the first time, and December brings both his first Christmas at Graceland and his draft notice.

**1958** Elvis is inducted on March 24. In August Elvis's mother, Gladys Presley, becomes ill. He returns home on August 12; Gladys dies on August 14, at age forty-six. In October Elvis arrives at an army base in Friedberg, West Germany, where he is stationed until March 1960.

**1959** Elvis visits Paris on a two-week leave. Elvis meets Priscilla in the fall of this year.

**1960** On March 5 Elvis is officially discharged from the army. Later that month he tapes a television special with Frank Sinatra; it airs in May. He goes on to score three number-one singles, one number-two album, and one number-one album before the end of the year.

**1961** February 25 is declared Elvis Presley Day in Tennessee. Elvis performs two shows at Ellis Auditorium to benefit more than thirty Memphis-area charities. In March he performs at Pearl Harbor, Hawaii, in a concert to benefit the building of a USS *Arizona* memorial. This turns out to be Elvis's last live performance until his 1968 television special.

**1962– 1969** Elvis continues making movies and recording movie soundtracks.

**1967** On May 1 Elvis and Priscilla are married in Las Vegas.

**1968** On February 1 Priscilla gives birth to Lisa Marie Presley. In mid-to-late June Elvis rehearses for his 1968 television special "Elvis." The actual taping is done on June 27–30. The show airs on December 3.

**1969** Elvis records in Memphis for the first time since 1955. These sessions yield, among other songs, "In the Ghetto," "Suspicious Minds," "Don't Cry, Daddy," and "Kentucky Rain." In March and April Elvis finishes up his last acting role, in the film *Change of Habit*. Beginning on July 31, Elvis opens up a triumphant four-week, fifty-seven-show engagement at the International Hotel in Las Vegas.

**1970** Elvis returns to Vegas in the early part of the year for another month-long engagement at the International Hotel; other extended gigs follow periodically in the next few years. Between February 27 and March 1 Elvis sells out six shows at the Houston Astrodome. In September Elvis begins his first tour since 1957. In December Elvis pays a visit to President Richard Nixon at the White House.

**1971** Elvis continues to perform, both in Las Vegas engagements and on the road. *Elvis: A Biography* by Jerry Hopkins is published in October. By early 1972 Elvis and Priscilla separate. She moves out on her own with Lisa Marie.

**1972** Highlights include the number-two pop hit "Burning Love" and four sold-out shows at New York's Madison Square Garden in June (a live album of one of the shows is rushed out nine days after it is recorded).

**1973** The "Aloha from Hawaii, via Satellite" special is performed and broadcast (mostly to the Pacific Rim) from Honolulu International Center Arena on January 14. It is seen on

American television on April 4. The album goes to number one on the Billboard pop album chart in May. In October Elvis and Priscilla officially divorce.

**1974–** Elvis continues to tour widely; these tours alternate with
**1977** Las Vegas engagements.

**1977** Elvis's last tour begins on June 17. His final concert is at Market Square Arena in Indianapolis on June 26. Elvis dies on August 16.

# DISCOGRAPHY

(Full-length albums only; early extended plays, greatest hits collections, and posthumous packages and box sets are not included.)

| Album title/year | Billboard chart peak position (for top twenty hits only) |
|---|---|
| *Elvis Presley* (1956) | 1 |
| *Elvis* (1956) | 1 |
| *Loving You* (1957) | 1 |
| *Elvis' Christmas Album* (1957) | 1 |
| *Elvis' Golden Records* (1958) | 3 |
| *King Creole* (1958) | 2 |
| *For LP Fans Only* (1959) | 19 |
| *A Date with Elvis* (1959) | |
| *50,000,000 Elvis Fans Can't Be Wrong, Elvis' Gold Records*, Vol. 2 (1959) | |
| *Elvis Is Back!* (1960) | 2 |
| *G. I. Blues* (1960) | 1 |
| *His Hand in Mine* (1961) | 13 |
| *Something for Everybody* (1961) | 1 |
| *Blue Hawaii* (1961) | 1 |
| *Pot Luck* (1962) | 4 |
| *Girls! Girls! Girls!* (1962) | 3 |
| *It Happened at the World's Fair* (1963) | 4 |
| *Elvis' Golden Records*, Vol. 3 (1963) | 3 |
| *Fun in Acapulco* (1963) | 3 |
| *Kissin' Cousins* (1964) | 6 |
| *Roustabout* (1964) | 1 |
| *Girl Happy* (1964) | 8 |
| *Elvis for Everyone!* (1965) | 10 |

| Album title/year | Billboard chart peak position (for top twenty hits only) |
|---|---|
| *Harum Scarum* (1965) | 8 |
| *Frankie and Johnny* (1966) | 20 |
| *Paradise, Hawaiian Style* (1966) | 15 |
| *Spinout* (1966) | 18 |
| *How Great Thou Art* (1967) | 18 |
| *Double Trouble* (1967) | |
| *Clambake* (1967) | |
| *Elvis' Gold Records*, Vol. 4 (1968) | |
| *Speedway* (1968) | |
| *Elvis* (1968) | 8 |
| *From Elvis in Memphis* (1969) | 13 |
| *Elvis in Person at the International Hotel* (1969) | |
| *From Memphis to Vegas, From Vegas to Memphis* (1969) | 12 |
| *On Stage—February 1970* (1970) | 13 |
| *Elvis—That's the Way It Is* (1970) | |
| *I'm 10,000 Years Old: Elvis Country* (1971) | 12 |
| *Love Letters from Elvis* (1971) | |
| *Elvis Sings the Wonderful World of Christmas* (1971) | |
| *Elvis Now* (1972) | |
| *He Touched Me* (1972) | |
| *Elvis as Recorded at Madison Square Garden* (1972) | 11 |
| *Elvis—Aloha from Hawaii, via Satellite* (1973) | 1 |
| *Elvis* (1973) | |
| *Raised on Rock* (1973) | |
| *Good Times* (1974) | |
| *Elvis Recorded Live on Stage in Memphis* (1974) | |
| *Promised Land* (1975) | |
| *Today* (1975) | |
| *From Elvis Presley Boulevard, Memphis, Tennessee* (1976) | |
| *Moody Blue* (1977) | 3 |

# FILMOGRAPHY

**Title/year of release**

**Studio**

1. *Love Me Tender* (1956) — Twentieth Century Fox
2. *Loving You* (1957) — Paramount
3. *Jailhouse Rock* (1957) — Metro-Goldwyn-Mayer
4. *King Creole* (1958) — Paramount
5. *G. I. Blues* (1960) — Paramount
6. *Flaming Star* (1960) — Twentieth Century Fox
7. *Wild in the Country* (1961) — Twentieth Century Fox
8. *Blue Hawaii* (1961) — Paramount
9. *Follow That Dream* (1962) — United Artists
10. *Kid Galahad* (1962) — United Artists
11. *Girls! Girls! Girls!* (1962) — Paramount
12. *It Happened at the World's Fair* (1963) — Metro-Goldwyn-Mayer
13. *Fun in Acapulco* (1963) — Paramount
14. *Kissin' Cousins* (1964) — Metro-Goldwyn-Mayer
15. *Viva Las Vegas* (1964) — Metro-Goldwyn-Mayer
16. *Roustabout* (1964) — Paramount
17. *Girl Happy* (1964) — Metro-Goldwyn-Mayer
18. *Tickle Me* (1965) — Allied Artists
19. *Harum Scarum* (1965) — Metro-Goldwyn-Mayer
20. *Frankie and Johnny* (1966) — United Artists
21. *Paradise, Hawaiian Style* (1966) — Paramount
22. *Spinout* (1966) — Metro-Goldwyn-Mayer
23. *Easy Come, Easy Go* (1967) — Paramount
24. *Double Trouble* (1967) — Metro-Goldwyn-Mayer
25. *Clambake* (1967) — United Artists
26. *Stay Away, Joe* (1968) — Metro-Goldwyn-Mayer
27. *Speedway* (1968) — Metro-Goldwyn-Mayer

| Title/year of release | Studio |
|---|---|
| 28. *Live a Little, Love a Little* (1968) | Metro-Goldwyn-Mayer |
| 29. *Charro!* (1969) | National General |
| 30. *The Trouble with Girls (and How to Get Into It)* (1969) | Metro-Goldwyn-Mayer |
| 31. *Change of Habit* (1969) | Universal |

**Concert films**

| | |
|---|---|
| 32. *Elvis—That's the Way It Is* (1970) | Metro-Goldwyn-Mayer |
| 33. *Elvis on Tour* (1972) | Metro-Goldwyn-Mayer |

# INDEX

**285**

Editor: Jeffrey Golick
Designer: Jordana Abrams
Graceland Director of Creative Services: Todd Morgan
Production Manager: Lou Bilka
Text: Adapted from the research and writing of Todd Morgan, with
  Laura Kath.

First edition
10  9  8  7  6  5  4  3  2  1

*Library of Congress Cataloging-in-Publication Data*
Elvis : his life in pictures
        p.      cm.
"A Tiny Folio."
Filmography: p. 279
Discography: p. 277
Includes index.
ISBN 0-7892-0157-7
  1. Presley, Elvis, 1935–1977—Homes and haunts—Tennessee—
Memphis.  2. Graceland Mansion (Memphis, Tenn.)  I. Title.
ML420.P96E356      1997
782.42166'092
[B]—dc21                                      96-40903